To Doug & Kelly —

yep — This is where your dad
(in-law) has spent the last
several years — I hope you
enjoy the read —

love,
Betty

Let's visit
LESOTHO

BETTY TONSING-CARTER

ACKNOWLEDGEMENTS

The Author and Publishers are grateful to the following organizations and individuals for permission to reproduce copyright illustrations in this book:

J. Allan Cash Photo Library; David Ambrose; The Hutchison Library; Rodwell King; The Lesotho National Development Corporation; The Lesotho Tourist Board; The Mansell Collection Ltd; The Ministry of Information and Broadcasting Lesotho; Tina Walkling.

The Author is particularly grateful to Brother Michael Mateka, Qenehelo Lekatsa Melvin, Meshu Mokitimi and David Ambrose for their help in the preparation of this book.

First published 1988

Published by
MACMILLAN PUBLISHERS LTD
Houndmills, Basingstoke, Hampshire RG21 2XS
and London
Companies and representatives
throughout the world

Designed and produced by Burke Publishing Company Limited
Pegasus House, 116-120 Golden Lane
London EC1Y 0TL, England.

Printed in Hong Kong

British Library Cataloguing in Publication Data
Tonsing-Carter, Betty
Let's visit Lesotho.—(Let's visit).
1. Lesotho—Social life and customs—
Juvenile literature
I. Title
968-1'603   DT786
ISBN 0-333-45508-8

Contents

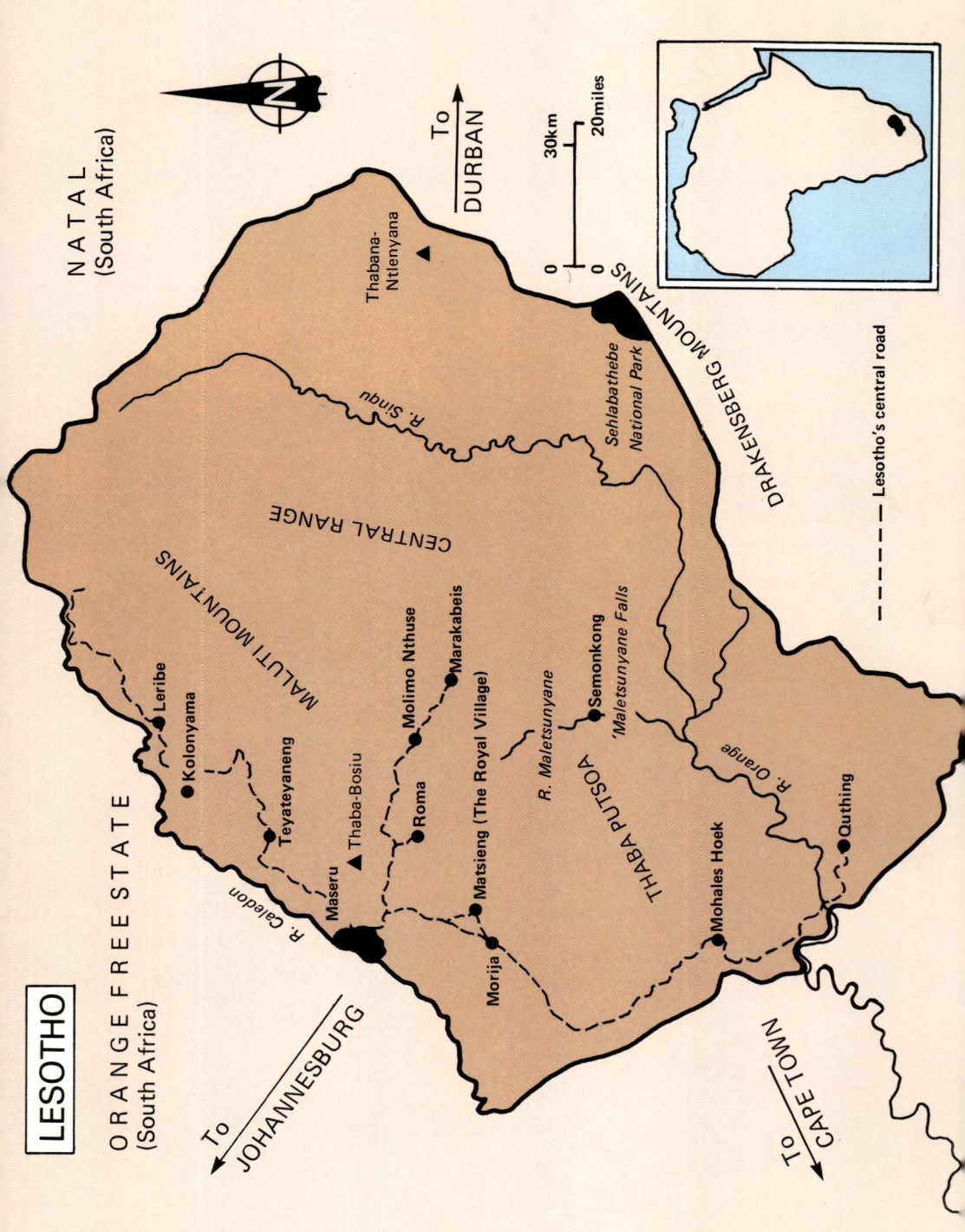

LESOTHO

NATAL
(South Africa)

ORANGE FREE STATE
(South Africa)

To JOHANNESBURG

To DURBAN

To CAPE TOWN

DRAKENSBERG MOUNTAINS

MALUTI MOUNTAINS

CENTRAL RANGE

THABA PUTSOA

Thabana-Ntlenyana

Sehlabathebe National Park

R. Singu

R. Caledon

R. Maletsunyane

R. Orange

Leribe

Kolonyama

Teyateyaneng

Maseru

Thaba-Bosiu

Roma

Matsieng (The Royal Village)

Molimo Nthuse

Marakabeis

Morija

Semonkong

'Maletsunyane Falls

Mohales Hoek

Quthing

30km
20miles

- - - - - Lesotho's central road

N

The Mountain Kingdom

Khotso-Pula-Nala—"Peace, Rain, Prosperity". These three important words greet people as they enter the Kingdom of Lesotho. Lesotho is a tiny African country located in the southern hemisphere, completely surrounded by the Republic of South Africa. The people are called Basotho (one person is a Mosotho) and the language is Sesotho.

Lesotho is a very mountainous country. Only fifteen per cent of the land is flat and fertile enough for farming. However, Lesotho is primarily an agricultural country. Every village farms at least one small area of land.

Lesotho has often been called the "Switzerland of Africa". It is the only country in the world with all its land rising more than one thousand metres (3,280 feet) above sea-level. The majestic mountains peak up to 3,482 metres (11,423 feet), and the 'Maletsunyane Falls at Semonkong are the highest single-drop falls in southern Africa.

Until recently, it was almost impossible to drive a vehicle

7

Lesotho is known as the "Switzerland of Africa". Its mountains can reach as high as 3,482 metres (11,423 feet)

through most of Lesotho. Travel across the mountains was either on foot or on horseback. Now, roads have been built through the mountains. However, driving is still very rough and hazardous, and thunderstorms often make the roads impassable. In addition, there may be a herd of cattle, sheep or goats around any narrow bend.

Although some thirty-five small landing-strips dot the rugged countryside, air travel is expensive. For this reason the local bus service is the usual form of travel between towns and villages.

Lesotho's high elevation accounts for its dry climate. The country is virtually free of the tropical diseases—such as malaria and bilharzia—found in other African countries, and the sun shines for more than three hundred days a year.

Summer (December to March) is considered the traditional rainy season. However, winter snow mixed with some rainfall helps provide adequate water supplies for Lesotho throughout the year. The mountains especially benefit from sufficient rain and snow, and water drains down, filling lowland rivers and streams. However, the western lowlands occasionally suffer periods of drought. The winter months (May to August) are followed by what is called Lesotho's ''fifth'' season—the ''dust'' season. During this period of several weeks, the wind howls and the air is filled with swirling dust clouds. Sometimes the sky looks pink as huge ''fields'' of dust travel slowly across the earth. Spring rains bring much needed relief and an end to the dust season.

Lesotho is one of the smallest countries in Africa with a total area of 30,355 square kilometres (11,720 square miles). It is

Many mountain roads, such as this one, are impassable to a normal vehicle and are challenging even to a tracked vehicle

similar in size to Belgium, or the American state of Maryland. Lesotho's population is about 1.4 million people, most of whom live in small towns and villages. Maseru, the modern capital city, is located on the western border, and is home to approximately 75,000 people.

The contrast between modern and traditional Africa is clearly seen when comparing Maseru with Lesotho's mountain villages. Visitors coming to Maseru are advised to travel light for Maseru's numerous stores display an amazing variety of commodities.

An earth satellite station located on a plateau just outside Maseru links Lesotho's telephones with the rest of the world by direct dialling, and the new international airport has moved Lesotho into the jet age. Even South African residents from

Herdboys with their sheep, cattle and angora goats

Snow on the Lesotho mountains

neighbouring farm districts flock to Maseru at weekends, taking advantage of the city's restaurants, cinemas, plays, craft centres, art exhibitions and other activities.

Yet 170 kilometres (105 miles) away, deep in the heart of the country and within the central mountain range, a bridle path is the only access to many small villages. There, modern civilization gives way to a biblical way of life. Barefoot shepherd boys tend their herds. Distant cow-bells carry an echo over treeless cliffs. Mothers walk great distances each day to fetch water, and children often do not attend school beyond Standard Seven (their seventh year at school). The only sign of the twentieth century is an occasional small aircraft flying overhead which is always a source of delight and wonderment to small

11

A view over Maseru

children far below. Winters are harsh and the mountain-tops
are often snowcapped. Even in the middle of summer, night-
time temperatures can plunge below freezing. In contrast,
residents in the lowlands often shed sweaters and jackets under
the bright sun of a warm midwinter day.

Lesotho's mountains seem stark. Yet it is here, sealed within
these mountains, that the country's true beauty and colour lie.
While Lesotho lacks the huge parks and wild game reserves
which attract visitors to other African countries, none can boast
the variety of scenes and visual contrasts which awaits the
traveller to Lesotho. Villages cloaked in smoke and the pink
misty dew of a winter's morning are best seen from horseback
on a steep mountain trail. Triple rainbows following violent
storms, fields of wild flowers stretched out like a thick carpet,

12

and friendly greetings from passing Basotho horsemen are all part of the typical scene. Lesotho's sapphire blue sky is full of puffy white clouds chasing across mountain peaks, and changes colour at the end of the day into radiant shades of red and orange. At night, brilliant stars appear, twinkling like diamonds spread out on black velvet.

The history of Lesotho goes back literally millions of years, and yet the country itself is very young. Skeletons, fossilized footprints of prehistoric dinosaurs and petrified wood are all signs of a life which has existed here since the dawn of time. The first human inhabitants were the Bushmen, or the San. They left many traces of their daily lives portrayed in rock paintings which are considered to be among the world's best.

The Basotho emerged as a nation between 1815 and 1820.

A rough track leading to a village. There are few paved roads in the mountains of Lesotho, so horses are essential for transport

Their leader, Moshoeshoe the Great, one of the young chiefs, was selected by a philosopher-prophet to become a just and peaceful ruler. Many wars were being fought by neighbouring clans. Moshoeshoe gathered together people who sought refuge in Lesotho's mountains. He built his kingdom from a mountain top called Thaba-Bosiu, or "mountain of the night", less than thirty kilometres (eighteen miles) from what is now Maseru. Thaba-Bosiu remains one of Lesotho's sacred places. Moshoeshoe is buried there, as are all Lesotho's principal chiefs.

Moshoeshoe was a skilled diplomat and warrior. While he preferred peace, he often had to fight in order to preserve his country's boundaries. Dutch settlers called Boers posed the most serious threat to his nation, by attempting to capture all the lowlands. Moshoeshoe appealed to the British monarch Queen Victoria, seeking protection. He asked that his tiny country (then called Basutoland) become like a "flea in the Queen's blanket". Lesotho became a British Protectorate in 1868.

Today, his great-great-great grandson, His Majesty King Moshoeshoe II, is Head of State. Lesotho gained its independence from Britain on 4 October 1966. The current system of law is based on a combination of local, Dutch and Roman law, and English Common Law.

The Basotho are a peaceful and proud people. Their cheerful nature is displayed by the colourful blankets they wear as their national dress.

A Basotho woman dressed in Lesotho's national dress—a colourful blanket thrown over one shoulder and secured with a safety-pin

Greetings are very important to the Basotho. They are never rushed, and a conversation will not take place until sufficient greetings have been exchanged. The Basotho never address someone by a first name unless they know the person well. Therefore, it is considered proper to address a man as *Ntate*, a married woman as *'M'e*, and an unmarried woman as *Aussi*. Basotho often first greet people with the word *Khotso*, meaning peace. *Khotso-Pula-Nala* is the national motto and is often used to close speeches on important occasions. An apostrophe mark (') before a word means that the first letter is pronounced twice.

The Royal Lesotho Mounted Police provide a great attraction at special ceremonies and parades. The mounted cavalry celebrated their centenary in 1972. This branch of the police force is of particular use in the rocky, mountainous regions—where the horse serves as a useful means of transportation—but is not often seen in urban areas.

As well as being responsible for the maintenance of law and order and the prevention of crime, the mounted police frequently appear at parades and special ceremonies such as the King's Birthday. The horses parade four abreast, the mounted troopers sitting upright in their saddles, their eyes looking straight ahead. Each trooper carries a tall staff with the colourful Royal Lesotho Mounted Police flag blowing in the breeze. The horses are beautifully groomed and well trained, and the troopers are expert riders.

Although Lesotho is small in size, it offers a surprising number of sparetime activities. Temperate winter and summer climates in the lowlands make outdoor sports possible throughout the year. The Basotho are keen football players, and tennis has recently become a popular sport. During the winter it is possible to ski in the mountains, while in summer, abundant rains swell the clear, flowing streams which are full of trout and bass. A fisherman equipped with sophisticated gear is no match for a young village boy's skill in catching fish with only string and a safety-pin.

One of the world's most difficult road races takes place each year across Lesotho's mountains. The race is called "The Roof of Africa", so named because of Lesotho's high altitude, and

A scene from the 1986 Lesotho International Open Tennis Championships. Tennis has recently become a popular sport in Lesotho

makes severe demands on an assortment of huge-wheeled vehicles and motor-cycles.

Lesotho is particularly proud of its traditional crafts. Its local pottery, colourful mohair tapestries and exquisite silver jewellery are sold all over the world.

While Maseru is a modern, cosmopolitan city, residents are often reminded of the country's mountain heritage. Occasionally a Basotho horseman will ride his horse swiftly through the centre of a town, and it is not uncommon to see horses hitched to a post near parked cars, or small groups of men and women performing traditional dances in front of a busy market. Lesotho is progressing quickly in a modern world. Yet this country which is vibrant with spectacular beauty is also rich in legend and folklore.

Lesotho's History

The history of Lesotho begins with the mountains which are fifty million years older than the Alps and cover eighty-five per cent of the country. Fossil footprints left by reptiles are thought to be over two hundred million years old.

A Bushman rock painting. The eland, a favourite animal of the Bushmen, was frequently featured in their rock paintings

The earliest known inhabitants were the Bushmen, or the San, many of whom lived in rock shelters. Not only were the San skilful hunters, they were also skilful painters and left evidence of their lives in rock paintings. The eland, a favourite animal, is often portrayed in these. It was once thought that the San

A portrait of
Moshoeshoe I as
a young warrior

did not fish. However, several of the rock paintings actually display people armed with spears in boats surrounding a shoal of fish.

The Basotho nation was formed from several clans. Symbols were used to distinguish each clan. One of the earliest clans, the Bakoena, chose a crocodile as their symbol. The crocodile is still a major symbol in Lesotho, and is often seen on Basotho blankets. It also forms part of a bronze monument in Maseru's city park which is dedicated to the Basotho who died during the First World War.

The first Sesotho-speaking people were the Bafokeng who lived in small groups and mixed freely with their San neighbours. By the late 1700s other clans also began to occupy small areas of Lesotho.

A prophet and rainmaker named Mohlomi travelled among the clans. In order to gain status and power, he married a chief's daughter wherever he went. He preached against evil and warned of a troubled period to come. On his travels, he met a young man by whom he was particularly impressed. He gave the young man an earring which was a sign that he had power to give orders and make others obey him. Mohlomi told the young man always to be fair and to choose peace instead of war. The young man's name was Lepoqo (he was later to become Moshoeshoe), and he was from the Bamokoteli branch of the Bakoena. Moshoeshoe would grow up to lead his nation and form the Kingdom of Lesotho.

In the early 1820s Shaka, Chief of the Zulu nation, was

waging bitter war against other nearby clans. The Zulu nation extended from the northeastern coast of South Africa—in what is now Natal—to the Drakensberg mountains which form Lesotho's eastern border. Many people fled from Zululand, to seek shelter in Lesotho's mountains. However, rather than move peacefully on their way, they stole cattle and grain, and fought with those they met. Because the roving warriors did not spare the time to sow and reap crops, their constant battles resulted in a famine. The famine was so severe that people turned to cannibalism in order to survive. This time, known to the Basotho as the *Lifaqana*, is the darkest period of Lesotho's history.

At this time Moshoeshoe was still a minor chief seeking a protected place for his people but surrounded by warring clans. His people had to move about quickly and, in time, tragedy befell the group. Moshoeshoe's grandfather, Peete, was captured and killed by the cannibals. Moshoeshoe finally chose for his fortress a secure mountain called Thaba-Bosiu, near his birthplace, and was able to defend it against many raids.

Eventually Moshoeshoe's power and peace-seeking influence won over the warring clans. Moshoeshoe was even able to forgive the cannibals for killing his grandfather. They were so taken by this act of justice that they became loyal citizens in Moshoeshoe's new nation. With time, Moshoeshoe's influence spread throughout Lesotho as he continued to gather scattered clans into a unified nation.

Lesotho's early history would not be complete without mention

A Basotho horseman, wearing the traditional Basotho blanket

of the Basotho horse. Today the horse is as much a part of
Lesotho as are the mountains. However, horses were not seen
in Lesotho until about 1830 when the Basotho people supposed
they were an odd-shaped ox without horns. The original Basotho
horse, or pony as it was commonly called, was brought to
southern Africa from Java (part of Indonesia) by the Dutch
settlers. Thus a new threat to Lesotho's peace was brought by
warriors on horseback. The Basotho were keen to possess some
of these new, swift animals. Members of the Griqua, once
enemies of Moshoeshoe, obtained several horses for him as a
sign of friendship. It soon became essential for each man to have
at least one horse, for it was a sign of poverty to be found walking
over the rough mountain paths instead of riding one of the sure-
footed ponies. It was on horseback that two of Moshoeshoe's

23

A mission house, first occupied in 1866

sons greeted the arrival of the first missionaries in Lesotho.

Members of the Paris Evangelical Missionary Society arrived in 1833. It was only later, in 1862, that the Roman Catholic missionaries arrived. The French missionaries were based in Morija, about twenty kilometres (thirteen miles) from Maseru. French and Sesotho were both spoken in the little settlement. The missionaries opened schools, and printed books in Sesotho, to help teach people to read. They also introduced potatoes, wheat, fruit trees and pigs to the Basotho. The missionaries' experience of the outside world was invaluable to Moshoeshoe

24

as settlers from the Orange Free State and the Cape Colony had begun to threaten his nation. Today these areas are all part of South Africa.

Lesotho's original western boundary once extended into the Orange Free State. The land was flat and fertile and was excellent farmland. However, the area also appealed to a group of white Dutch settlers who were moving up from Cape Town in search of new homelands. These people were called Boers and were part of the Voortrekker movement—first European settlers of the Transvaal and Orange Free State. They opposed the British who governed Cape Town. To show their opposition to British domination, they developed their own language called Afrikaans, which is still widely spoken throughout South Africa. The Voortrekkers and their descendants are known today as Afrikaaners or Boers.

The land adjoining Moshoeshoe's western boundary was ruled by the British government from the Cape Colony. Many disputes broke out over which was Lesotho's land and which belonged to the Cape Colony. Several battles took place, but Moshoeshoe's small army was always able to defeat attempts to take over his land. Moshoeshoe also showed great skill as a diplomat. Wishing for peace not war, he appealed to the British for mercy, and asked not to be considered an enemy.

Eventually, the British decided to give up sovereignty over the Orange Free State and this whole area was handed over to the Boers. The Boers were determined not to give up this fertile land to the Basotho and the First Basotho-Boer War took place

25

in 1858. The Basotho won, and the fighting stopped. The Second Basotho-Boer War took place in 1865. This time the Boers sought help from other Voortrekkers in the Cape and Transvaal areas. Their enlarged army proved stronger than the Basotho. Moshoeshoe was forced to sign over much of his western land in the agreement called the ''Peace of Thaba-Bosiu''. The Boers agreed that they would live in peace with the Basotho. However, in 1867, another war broke out in which the Boers were stronger than ever and Moshoeshoe's army was forced to retreat to Thaba-Bosiu.

Moshoeshoe appealed to Queen Victoria for British protection. The British still ruled the Cape Colony area and agreed to help the Basotho against the Boers. On 12 March 1868, Lesotho became a British Protectorate. At that time, Lesotho was called Basutoland; a name which remained until Independence. Two years later, Moshoeshoe died at the age of eighty. He was succeeded by his son Letsie.

In 1871, Lesotho ceased to be a Protectorate, or Crown Colony, and was controlled from the British-ruled Cape Colony. The Cape Colony wanted to administer the same laws in Lesotho as it applied to other African British colonies. In 1879 it passed a ''Peace Preservation Act''. Under this Act, all firearms were to be surrendered. The Basotho refused, and in the Gun War of 1880 to 1881, they once again proved themselves to be strong fighters. The Act was eventually repealed. By 1884, Britain had once again resumed direct responsibility for Lesotho as a British Protectorate. The Basotho had demonstrated that they were a
26

The grave of Moshoeshoe I, the tribal chief who founded the kingdom of Lesotho, and died in 1870 at the age of eighty

strong nation and had won the right to be governed separately from other colonies.

The Basotho developed their own form of local government. The *pitso*, or open-air assembly, was used by the principal chiefs to discuss important issues with their people. The *lekhotla*, or court of the village elders, was used for settling minor disputes. The *pitso* is still used today in villages, towns and cities for discussing major issues.

The years leading up to Independence were not a good period for Lesotho. Between 1868 and 1966, Lesotho was affected by two world wars and a world-wide economic depression. A terrible drought · from 1932 to 1933 brought starvation throughout the country. Lesotho's limited farmlands were

27

overcultivated and overgrazed, leading to severe soil erosion which still exists today. Men sought employment in the mines of South Africa, while their wives stayed in Lesotho and continued raising their families, in addition to working in the fields or finding some other means of income.

At the same time, a new change was taking place across the African continent. African colonies were regaining their independence. Lesotho also struggled for independence. On 4 October 1966, ninety-eight years of British rule ended. The kingdom of Moshoeshoe the Great was restored to his great-great-great-grandson Moshoeshoe II as the Kingdom of Lesotho.

Lesotho's Government

The chieftainship system was created by Moshoeshoe I. He organized his kingdom into a series of areas and placed a chief in charge of each one. The first three Basotho chiefs were Moshoeshoe's brothers; and later, the four sons of his senior wife, 'Mamahato, were made chiefs.

In time, as the Basotho nation grew, the larger areas were divided under a principal chief called a ward chief. These smaller sections were then further subdivided under area chiefs, and a village headman was in his turn made responsible to each area chief.

Today, there are twenty-two ward chiefs, nineteen of whom are direct descendants of Moshoeshoe I or one of his brothers. These chiefs are generally known as *Bara ba Moshoeshoe*, which means the "Sons of Moshoeshoe". There are also 508 area chiefs and 637 village headmen, most of whom are also direct descendants of Moshoeshoe's family. It is often said in Lesotho that the people of the Basotho nation are of one large family.

29

The twenty-two ward chiefs form the College of Chiefs and are responsible for naming the King's successor.

During Lesotho's period as a British Crown Colony, Britain assisted in administrative affairs. It collected taxes, maintained law and order and helped ensure that the Basotho lived in peace with their Boer neighbours.

The British administrators supported Lesotho's traditional system of government. The Paramount Chief (a royal

A photograph of Moshoeshoe I, taken in about 1860

A *pitso*, or open-air assembly, where everyone is free to express an opinion on local affairs — a truly democratic event

descendant of Moshoeshoe) and the ward chiefs were responsible for the day-to-day administration of the Basotho's traditional affairs. The Paramount Chief's headquarters were at Matsieng, the royal birthplace.

Today, the *pitso* is central to the Basotho's way of government. There is complete freedom of expression in a *pitso* which may be a small village gathering or a large national assembly. The *pitso* is still regarded as the most democratic means of governing local affairs.

Lesotho's judicial system includes a Supreme Court, Court

of Appeals, Resident Magistrate's Court and a number of regional courts.

In 1965 Lesotho held its first national elections. Chief Leabua Jonathan became the first Prime Minister of the Kingdom of Lesotho. In January 1986 a change in the government system took place. All law-making and executive authority was vested in the Paramount Chief, King Moshoeshoe II. The King is advised by the Military Council and assisted by the Council of Ministers whom he appoints.

Education, Health and Religion

EDUCATION

Formal education in Lesotho first began with the Christian missionaries. They established primary schools all over the country and, by 1930, there were over 800 primary schools in Lesotho, with almost every child within walking distance of a school.

The early mission schools emphasized the importance of reading and writing. As a result, Lesotho has one of the highest literacy rates in Africa. More than fifty per cent of the adult population is able to read and write Sesotho. Additionally, while most primary schools teach in Sesotho, English is generally used after Standard Five.

Today, the Roman Catholic Church, Lesotho Evangelical Church and Anglican Church run ninety-six per cent of all primary schools in Lesotho.

Children attending a mission or government primary school do not pay school fees. However, parents must pay for school

33

An arithmetic class at a village school

books and uniforms. Most primary schools have a garden. The children help take care of the gardens and the vegetables they grow are an important part of their daily diet.

Children who complete Standard Seven (their seventh year at school) may enter a three-year Junior Certificate course or a five-year High School course leading to the Cambridge Overseas School Certificate. Maseru's Machabeng High School is an international school offering a wide range of examination subjects.

Education is very important to the Basotho. Each year 50,000 children are admitted into the first year and schools are often very crowded. However, only four out of ten children complete

Standard Seven and of the children who start High School, only one in ten completes the course. The main reason for so many children leaving school is poverty. Secondary schools are not free, and few parents can afford the school fees. This occurs most often among children who live in the mountain villages where many of the children are needed for chores at home. Young boys are expected to tend to the family's cattle, sheep and goats. Young girls help their mothers with household chores and take care of smaller children in the family. The government wants to make school courses more meaningful for these particular children. It has introduced practical studies in mathematics, agriculture and home economics to help them

Basotho schoolchildren

become useful members in their local community. In addition to serving social needs, the government is also keen for the children to develop a love for their country and an appreciation of its national heritage.

There are over seven thousand primary and secondary school teachers in Lesotho, many of whom are from international volunteer programmes. The National Teachers Training College was opened in 1975 to help train local teachers and it has nine hundred full-time students. An additional five hundred teachers are taking part-time courses. The three-year course includes one year of teaching practice. During this year, the students work in the schools alongside regular teachers. This is a very valuable year as the students return to their course-work with a better understanding of the many practical problems they must deal with as professional teachers.

As a growing nation, Lesotho needs skilled technicians. There are several technical training institutes and co-operative schools that offer a wide range of practical training courses. These include motor mechanics, carpentry, stonemasonry, medical laboratory training, and electrical and mechanical engineering. Lesotho's modern telephone system and international airport have also created opportunities for special training in telecommunications and civil aviation.

Lesotho's economy is still largely based on agriculture and small farms. Students attending classes at the Thaba Khupa Ecumenical Institute learn improved methods of vegetable, fruit and poultry production. These skills are useful for developing agricultural projects in their home villages. Students who want to learn more about agriculture and rural management attend the Lesotho Agricultural College.

Lesotho is particularly proud of its National University. The university first began as the Catholic University College in 1945. At that time, courses were taught in a converted primary school and there were just five students and four teachers! Later the school was renamed Pius XII College and admitted students from all parts of southern and central Africa.

The neighbouring countries of Botswana and Swaziland also wanted to provide a university education for their people. As a result, the University of Botswana, Lesotho and Swaziland was formed in 1964. The main college was in Lesotho, and Botswana and Swaziland opened campuses in 1971. Lesotho's campus is located in Roma, about thirty-five kilometres (twenty-two miles) from Maseru. Roma was named for *Ba-Roma*, which means "place of the Roman Catholics". It is in a picturesque valley amid the foothills of the Maluti Mountains. Beautiful sandstone buildings form much of the campus and Roma's village has grown to house the increasing number of departments and administrative staff. Over the years many new buildings have been added to Roma's original campus. They are modern but they have been designed to blend in with the original architecture and with the numerous trees that adorn the campus.

The Roma campus became the National University of Lesotho in 1975. Today, it has over eleven hundred students. The teachers are from twenty different countries, a fact which

In some villages sorghum is stored in traditional beehive-shaped granary baskets known as *seisus*. Lesotho's economy is still largely based on agriculture but nevertheless relatively few modern farming and storage techniques have been introduced

makes it a truly international university. A second campus was recently opened in Maseru for adult education.

Students attending the university are proud of their achievement. The students from the rural villages, especially, had to overcome many hardships just to meet the requirements necessary for admission. King Moshoeshoe II is the university's Chancellor. Each year students are awarded degrees in law, humanities, science, economics, social studies and education.

Another form of education in Lesotho is "Outward

Bound''—one of thirty-three international programmes that gives people an opportunity to take on physical and mental challenges. Outward Bound programmes are conducted out of doors in completely natural surroundings. Lesotho was chosen for the courses because of its rugged environment and wide open spaces. It is also easy for people to travel to Lesotho from all parts of southern and central Africa. Courses include rock-climbing, canoeing, camping and hiking and are very popular with people of all ages. Young people are anxious to learn new skills in a school without walls, while adults want to rediscover the spirit of adventure missing from their hectic workdays.

HEALTH

Although Lesotho has long welcomed modern health services, many Basotho still rely on traditional healers when a member of the family is ill. Traditional medicine remains an important part of Basotho culture. The people believe that good health is a natural human condition. The Sesotho word for health is *bophelo* which, literally translated means ''living well''. A Mosotho may choose to see a traditional healer rather than a doctor for a very serious illness if he believes that the illness has been caused by the anger or unhappiness of an ancestor. Part of the herbal medicine may include washing the body in the blood of a slain animal. This ceremony is used to thank the ancestors for recovery from a long illness. It is believed that the magical powers of the traditional healer can cure an illness and this belief is part of the cure. Similarly, many doctors believe

39

that a patient's mental attitude is an important part of recovery from a serious illness.

However, sometimes traditional medicine can be harmful. Diarrhoea is a very serious problem among small children in Lesotho. Many children die from this illness which is caused by bad water or food. According to modern medicine, a child with diarrhoea should drink a lot of fluids; in particular, good water. Yet traditional healing demands that the child's body rid itself of the poison that caused the diarrhoea. In this respect, traditional and modern medicine disagree.

A traditional healer whose treatments include herbal remedies. Traditional medicine remains an important part of Basotho culture

Villagers attending a talk on health care

Lesotho respects the cultural heritage of traditional healing, but also recognizes the need for modern health care.

The government has trained thousands of health workers to help solve health problems. These people live in villages and work with the families and with traditional healers. Plays and puppet shows performed in the villages are a popular way to teach important health issues (such as proper sanitation and nutrition), as are radio programmes and posters in the towns.

There are several health clinics scattered throughout Lesotho. Many of them still cannot be reached by road due to the steep mountains. The health clinics communicate with the nearest hospital by radio telephone. There is also the Lesotho Flying Doctor service which helps bring medicine to these clinics and which flies critically ill patients to hospital.

People waiting outside a village clinic for a visit from the flying doctor. Lesotho now recognizes the need for modern medicine

Lesotho has several government and mission hospitals. The main hospital, Queen Elizabeth II, is in Maseru. International organizations such as the United Nations World Health Organization and the Save the Children Fund have helped provide Lesotho with doctors, nurses, medical equipment and medicines. Immunization against measles, polio, diphtheria, whooping cough, tetanus and tuberculosis have helped save many children from early death. Lesotho still does not have a medical college. Its doctors and dentists are trained in other African countries, in Europe or in the United States.

42

RELIGION

The influence of Christian mission schools on Lesotho's society has enabled most Basotho to read and write. However, religion also plays a significant role apart from education, and commands great respect. For example, it is very important for a political party or politician in Lesotho to be associated with an accepted religion. Almost forty per cent of the Basotho are Roman Catholics, and many others belong to the Lesotho Evangelical Church and the Anglican Church. However, people of all religious backgrounds are free to practise their faith in Lesotho.

There is a strong feeling among some Basotho that the early missionaries tried to eliminate certain Basotho customs and

The church at the National University of Lesotho

rituals which they considered to be heathen practices. Today, however, church involvement in Lesotho is more sensitive to Lesotho's culture. Many clergymen and nuns are Basotho, and they have helped the churches understand and appreciate Lesotho's traditional heritage.

Village and Town Life

Lesotho is primarily a rural country. The village is still regarded as the true home of a Masotho, even if he has moved away to a town or city. Villages are generally named after a person, often the founding chief or headman.

Many villages consist of only a few homes, or *rondavels*. A *rondavel* is a round hut made of mud and stones with a thatched roof. Some homes are not round, but are built in a rectangular shape and have a tin roof. Sometimes a creative owner will decorate the walls of the home in a flower or geometric design. Often there are fenced areas for livestock (called *kraals*) close to the homes. Small gardens and peach trees frequently surround the villages. The Basotho are very neat people and their homes, although small, are kept tidy and clean.

Most of the cooking is done in three-legged pots outside the *rondavel*. Since wood is scarce, dried cow-dung is generally burned as a source of fuel. Maize is the important food in the daily diet. A popular drink is *joala*, the locally brewed beer. Small

45

Rondavels **made of mud and stones, with a thatched roof. Village homes are kept tidy and clean and tend to be built close together, adding to a strong sense of community and family**

flags are flown high from a stick to indicate when the *joala* is available.

Small villages do not have electricity or plumbing. In order to preserve good health and prevent unnecessary disease, the government has supported a large number of sanitation efforts to construct latrines and establish clean water supplies.

Children born in the villages are often given names which relate to their birth. Examples of such names are *Tseleng*, ''born on the roadside'', *Paseka*, ''born at Easter'', *Sefako*, ''born during a hailstorm'', and *'Malehola*, ''mother of weeds''—given to a girl born at weeding time. Christian Basotho babies are baptized and also given a Christian name, such as that of an early saint. A mother generally carries her baby with her on her back, secured by a blanket wrapped around her upper body.

Everyone in the village has work to do, even the small children. Boys learn to be herdboys at the age of five and often a young herdboy does not start school until he is twelve years old. The herds are his responsibility and he can only start school when a younger brother is old enough to take his place. Girls usually begin school when they are seven years old. As a result,

Young Basotho herdboys with their sheep. Many boys are unable to start school until they are twelve years old or when a younger brother can take over their job looking after the herd

they receive more years of schooling than boys, and Lesotho women are therefore often better educated than the men.

Young girls help their mothers clean the home and wash clothes. They learn how to fetch water and carry it in buckets on their heads. Older children are expected to help take care of the younger children and it is not uncommon to see older brothers and sisters carrying the younger ones on their backs.

According to traditional law, everyone is responsible for the behaviour of children. If a passing stranger sees that a herdboy is allowing his cattle to eat someone else's crops, he is expected to scold the child and correct his behaviour. If he fails to intervene, the stranger could be sued or fined.

The Basotho are law-abiding people and have a local system for handling disputes. Every village has a *lekhotla*, or court of the village chief. The *lekhotla* is usually situated under a tree near the *kraal* for the chief's cattle. The chief and his advisors hear evidence and settle problems that cannot be settled within the family.

According to tradition, all land in Lesotho was held in trust by the King. The land was allocated to area chiefs who in turn could give land to another person. Land could not be bought or sold. However, as the nation grew, more people started to settle in urban areas. They wanted to build homes which they could own. New industries also required land for development. Lesotho needed a legislation that would respect traditional rights but also allow for new growth. The Land Act 1979 and the Town and Country Planning Act 1980 created a new lease system for commercial and residential use. While all land is still owned by the Royal Family, these Acts ensure that sufficient land is available for urban development.

Approximately ten per cent of Lesotho's population live in urban areas. Maseru is the largest of these and, like the larger towns, is situated in the western lowlands.

Maseru was established in 1869. It lies on the Caledon River which marks the border between Lesotho and the Republic of South Africa. The site was selected as the administrative capital by the British who realized that its location on the river made it a natural trading centre.

By 1966, Maseru's population had risen to fourteen thousand. Cars had replaced horses, and electricity had replaced candles, but little else had changed in Maseru during the 1900s except for a four-kilometre (two-and-a-half-mile) stretch of road. This was paved through the centre of the town in 1947. The road was called Kingsway in celebration of a royal visit by Britain's King George VI and Queen Elizabeth. Kingsway and an even smaller stretch of road, leading to the railway station, remained the only tarred roads in Lesotho until 1966.

Even in the 1970s, while no longer a sleepy village, Maseru still bore little resemblance to a commercial city. However, today the contrast is phenomenal. Virtually all the roads are tarred and continue on to link all the major towns in the western lowlands. New traffic lights, which were first introduced in 1978, are being constantly erected to regulate the increasing amount of traffic. Downtown high-rise office complexes share the skyline

49

with huge grain siloes and manufacturing facilities in the modern industrial area located close to the centre of Maseru. There is a wide choice of restaurants, supermarkets and cinemas. Beautiful old sandstone structures that were once private homes are being converted into chic speciality stores, and street cafés, with tables shaded under wide colourful umbrellas, add a cosmopolitan flair to the city.

The King's Palace is in the middle of Maseru. Although the King's home is not open to the public, an auditorium in the Palace grounds frequently features plays, music festivals and other similar entertainment.

At one time the people of Maseru would drive for over an hour to Bloemfontein in South Africa in order to buy commodities not found in Lesotho. Today, that is not necessary. On the contrary, tourists from neighbouring countries and abroad come to Maseru to the comfort of one of its several luxury hotels. Weekends are full of craft, art and photographic exhibitions, plays, sports tournaments and even polo games.

A new international airport, the Moshoeshoe I, has recently opened outside Mazenod, which is about twenty kilometres (twelve miles) from Maseru. The airport will enable Lesotho to use short-range jet traffic without having to stop in South Africa for refuelling.

The life of an urban Basotho is quite different from the life of those who live in rural areas. Larger homes with electricity,

A village chief, dressed in western clothes but wearing the traditional Basotho hat

plumbing, and household appliances allow for more leisure time. Many families have a television, and night-time viewing has replaced story-telling and traditional games. Parents often work away from home, leaving their children in the care of a maid or older relative. The traditional blanket has been replaced by modern business suits and dresses.

Older Basotho are concerned that the younger, urbanized generation will never learn to appreciate Lesotho's traditional culture. They feel that legends and folklore may be forgotten, especially as European and American fashions, music and trends have captured the imagination of Lesotho's youth. This problem is not unique to Lesotho. It is a problem shared by all developing countries, anxious both to preserve their traditional heritage and progress with the modern, changing world.

Kingsway, the main street of Maseru. The tall building in the background is the Lesotho Bank Centre

Lesotho's extended family structure is probably the key to preserving its traditional heritage. Most Basotho can draw a line from their present family to Moshoeshoe I and his family. This has created a special national pride.

Another factor in preserving Lesotho's heritage is respect for elders. Children are taught that they are never too old to respect and obey their older relatives. An appreciation for one's cultural heritage seems to grow with age. Nevertheless, the elders will make certain that their younger generation never forget Lesotho's cultural heritage and proud history.

Industry and Development

According to the United Nations, Lesotho is among the poorest countries in the world. Although agriculture is the major economic activity, only fifteen per cent of the land is suitable for large-scale agricultural production. Water, people and scenery have often been identified as Lesotho's only useful resources. The lack of employment has forced many Basotho to work outside Lesotho, mainly in South Africa. Each year, twenty thousand Basotho enter South Africa's labour force.

Fifty per cent of Lesotho's male working population work in South Africa's gold and diamond mines. They are away from their homes for weeks and months at a time which means that their children grow up without their fathers. Miners only return home permanently when they retire or are disabled. Tuberculosis—once unheard of in Lesotho—is now a major health problem among returning Basotho miners.

As much as sixty per cent of Lesotho's gross national income is based on foreign aid. Large international donor organizations, such as the United Nations, have spent millions of dollars in foreign aid assistance to help Lesotho become more self-sufficient.

Lesotho is largely dependent on South Africa for food, clothing and other household items. In fact, Lesotho has a very high import market for most goods. This has been both a benefit and a problem. On one hand, Lesotho's trade with South Africa means that the country benefits by having access to a wide range of commodities. On the other hand, this dependency has resulted from Lesotho's lack of manufacturing resources prior to Independence.

Industry was practically non-existent before 1966. The only industries were two small printing works in Morija which employed less than one hundred people. Lesotho was largely underdeveloped. There was no means of transportation or communication outside Maseru. Villages and towns had no electricity. Water was abundant, but less than one per cent was used for irrigation and domestic consumption. The only agriculture consisted of small village farms.

One of the first initiatives the government undertook following independence was to establish the Lesotho National Development Corporation (LNDC). The purpose of the LNDC is to encourage investment in Lesotho and to assist in the development of industry and commerce. Although Lesotho is still struggling as a developing country, the LNDC has achieved tremendous success in attracting large businesses to open facilities there. Sufficient jobs have still not been created to

An early picture (taken in about 1863) of the printing works in Morija, Lesotho's only industry before independence

replace employment in the mines of South Africa, but growing industries are offering new opportunities for many younger Basotho men and women.

The LNDC makes generous offers to new investors. These include duty-free access to southern African markets, loans and training grants. Moreover, preferential treatment is given to Lesotho exporters in the EEC (the European Economic Community) and other world markets.

Most of these new businesses are based in Maseru. However, one of Lesotho's main exports is wool and woollen textiles. The wool is obtained from small herds of family-owned goats and sheep in the little villages throughout Lesotho. Government-sponsored co-operatives, offering both financial and practical aid, have been established in several rural areas to assist small business workshops in cleaning and spinning wool into usable yarn. This is used by Lesotho's handicraft industries to make tapestries, sweaters and other articles of clothing which are sold to European and American markets.

The majority of people employed in the craft workshops and co-operatives are women, whose salaries are critical to their families. Women play a major role in preserving Lesotho's traditional culture and are important to the country's overall development. Basotho women hold key positions in Lesotho's government, own several small businesses and serve as officers in many different organizations.

Spinning at a government-sponsored co-operative. The wool comes from small family-owned herds

The local manufacture of footwear, clothing, beverages, tinned fruit and vegetables, meat, flour and wheat products and drugs has helped further reduce Lesotho's dependence on South African products.

Tourism is one of Lesotho's main industries. Until recently, the majority of Lesotho's tourists were from South Africa. The main attractions were the gambling casinos because gambling is illegal in South Africa. In Europe and the United States and more recently in the Far East and Australia, the Lesotho Tourist Board has been actively promoting travel to Lesotho. Stunning

Weaving in a craft workshop. Women play a major role in preserving Lesotho's traditional crafts

Lesotho Flour Mills, Maseru. Manufacturing concerns such as this are helping to reduce Lesotho's dependence on South African products

pictures of Lesotho's scenery and colourful handicrafts are used as excellent publicity for promoting tourism.

In an effort to encourage the development of small businesses, the Basotho Enterprises Development Corporation (BEDCO) was established to provide loans, workshop facilities and business counselling to entrepreneurs. BEDCO has small-scale trade and manufacturing centres in Maseru and other urban areas.

Transportation and telecommunications are critical to Lesotho's economic development. New roads are being built

59

**A furniture factory
sponsored by BEDCO
in Maseru**

through mountains, thereby creating routes for goods and
linking towns together for the first time. The Moshoeshoe I
International Airport also serves as an important link between
Lesotho and other countries within the African and European
continents. Longer-range air transport, combined with enlarged
air cargo capability, will enable Lesotho to expand its export
trade. For example, fresh produce grown in Lesotho's summer
months can be flown under refrigeration direct to northern
countries experiencing winter temperatures.

The advanced telecommunications project includes a highly
technical, modern microwave radio-telephone network, earth
satellite station and switching centre. The telephone has bridged

the gap between the towns and villages. It has given businesses the opportunity to develop in the rural areas and has helped attract new businesses to urban areas. It has also provided a much-needed means of communication between families separated by long distances, and has enabled migrant workers to stay in touch with their families.

Over half of Lesotho's calls are to other southern African countries. Prior to the existence of Lesotho's new telephone network, these calls had to be routed through South Africa, which in turn collected most of the long-distance revenue. The new system provides a direct link with whichever country is

The earth satellite station which links Lesotho's telephone network with the rest of the world

required, and Lesotho is able to keep the extra revenues brought about by this telephone traffic.

Water has been called Lesotho's "white gold". While the lowlands occasionally experience periods of drought, the mountains generally benefit from abundant rains. In contrast, the vast farmlands of neighbouring South Africa often suffer from rain shortages. Millions of dollars and many years of planning have gone into the massive Highland Water Project scheme. The project will produce hydroelectric power for Lesotho and provide dams for water to be sold to South Africa. In a country with few available resources, this project could ultimately be the major boost Lesotho needs to build a strong economy.

Lesotho's banking system consists of the Central Bank of Lesotho, three commercial banks (Barclay's Bank International, the Standard Bank and the Lesotho National Bank), and two other institutions concerned with agricultural and housing finance. Lesotho's commercial banks are computerized and provide electronic banking services with other banks around the world. Lesotho used the South African *rand* as its national currency until January 1980, when it introduced its own currency called the *loti* (plural:*maloti*). Both the *rand* and the *loti* are accepted in Lesotho.

Lesotho's Varied and Colourful Attractions

Lesotho's year-round sunshine makes it a pleasant place to visit at any time of the year. With each season, the country offers a kaleidoscope of colours. A flight over Lesotho reveals unspoiled mountain scenery, deep rivers, sparkling streams and shimmering waterfalls. During the spring (late August to the

Pink peach blossom adds colour to Lesotho's barren countryside in the spring which begins in late August

end of October) trees covered in pink peach-blossom can be seen across the brown terrain. In summer, the mountains are surrounded by emerald green fields. In the autumn, the smoke from the villages casts purple shadows against brilliant sunsets; and in the winter, the mountains are covered by a blanket of snow.

Almost three hundred varieties of birds have been identified in Lesotho. These include the rare Giant Kingfisher, and the huge Lammergeyer which has a wing span of two and a half metres (eight feet). Lesotho is also famous for its spiral aloe— or *Aloe polyphylla*—which can be found nowhere else in the world. This large plant has five separate leaves which grow in clockwise and anti-clockwise spirals. Long tubular orange flowers grow from the aloe's centre. At one time this plant was in danger of becoming extinct as many people were digging it up to put in their gardens. Large plants were uprooted by the village women who carried them into town on their heads to sell as novelty items. The aloe is now protected by the Lesotho Protection and Preservation Commission, and an Act passed in 1970 prohibits its removal and export.

Lesotho is an ideal place for hiking, and there are also several trails throughout the countryside for pony-trekking. The Basotho pony is a sturdy animal that can live on veld grass alone and moves with incredible ease over a rough trail. The Basotho Pony Project aims to improve the breeding stock of the Basotho pony by breeding local mares with Connemara stallions imported from

The *Aloe polyphylla*—
the spiral aloe—a
protected plant which
grows only in Lesotho

Ireland. Basotho ponies are available for rides that can range from an afternoon trek to a nearby waterfall, to a camping excursion which takes several days. When hiking or riding through the countryside, it is possible to camp overnight in a village. However, permission must always be obtained first from the village chief.

Since Lesotho now has several good tarred roads, it is possible to travel to many places of interest in an ordinary motor car. One such place is Lesotho's most important historical site, Thaba Bosiu—the mountain on which Moshoeshoe I defended and built his nation.

65

Typical Lesotho scenery seen from one of the new roads which now make it possible to travel to many places by car

Morija was Lesotho's first settlement. It was founded in 1833 by French missionaries. Today Morija is the home of the headquarters of the Lesotho Evangelical Church. The Morija Museum houses dinosaur fossils, jewellery, traditional ornaments, clothing and dishes—including an 1850 Parisian tea service which was originally used by Moshoeshoe I while entertaining guests.

Matsieng is six kilometres (four miles) east of Morija and is the King's Royal Village. It is possible to visit the King's home if a prior request is made.

Several large craft centres are also within easy driving distance of Maseru. Teyateyaneng—generally referred to as "TY"— and Leribe have a number of pottery and tapestry workshops

66

and galleries. A large pottery centre is located between TY and Leribe, from which Kolonyama pottery is exhibited and sold throughout the world.

The *Molimo Nthuse* Lodge offers a beautiful weekend resort for Maseru's residents. *Molimo Nthuse* means "God help me". The Lodge is located fifty-five kilometres (thirty-four miles) from Maseru on a tarred road, and lies by the Makhaleng River. Its easy access from Maseru attracts hiking and fishing enthusiasts from the city. Pan-fried trout is a speciality of the lodge.

It is a more difficult journey for a standard car on the way to Semonkong. The name Semonkong means "place of smoke". Rocks and flooded bridges pave the way to the 'Maletsunyane

An aerial view of the town of Leribe, the centre in which several pottery and tapestry workshops are located

Examples of Kolonyama pottery

Falls which, at 192 metres (630 feet), are the highest single-drop falls in southern Africa.

A heavy-duty four-wheel-drive vehicle—such as a Land Rover—is necessary for a trip to the Sehlabathebe National Park which is about 375 kilometres (233 miles) from Maseru. The park is located on Lesotho's eastern border, and is deep in the highest mountain region. Getting to Sehlabathebe itself is half the fun. The eastern region contains the most spectacular of Lesotho's mountains. However, the narrow passes and steep cliffs are not for the faint-hearted.

68

More than five hundred sets of fossil prints have been found in Lesotho, some of which have been traced back to the dinosaur. Many sites are near Mohale's Hoek, which is 128 kilometres (80 miles) from Maseru. Some five thousand Bushman rock paintings have also been identified in Lesotho. However, the paintings are beginning to erode due to time, weather and vandalism. These paintings are now protected by the Lesotho Protection and Preservation Commission.

Since it requires a long treacherous hike to reach many of the sites, they are thus protected from a large number of the general public. By contrast, the *Ha Baroana* site, or "place of the Bushmen", is near Roma. The reserve is fenced in and is open to the public.

'Maletsunyane Falls at Semonkong—at 192 metres (630 feet), this is the highest single-drop waterfall in southern Africa

Lesotho is one of the most active southern African countries in international sports. The Lesotho Sports Council plays host to teams from Europe, the United States, South America, New Zealand and Australia, as well as other African countries. Soccer is the national sport and is played everywhere; both on large fields and in small villages. Lesotho is the only southern African country which belongs to the "Federation Internationale de Football" (FIFA). Basotho players are allowed to compete in the world cup competition held every four years. The Sports Council has also sent boxers to the Olympic Games.

Tennis is a more recently adopted sport. It is called Lesotho's "Royal Sport" as His Majesty King Moshoeshoe II is himself a keen player. The Basotho have demonstrated their competitive spirit in several regional tennis tournaments.

An example of Bushman rock paintings

A soccer match—soccer is Lesotho's national sport

One need not be a professional or even a top-flight amateur to enjoy the wide range of sports activities in Lesotho. There is something for everyone, whether it is tennis, swimming, football, jogging, lawn bowls, badminton, volleyball, ten-pin bowling, mountaineering, fishing, camping, skiing, boxing, cricket or horseriding.

Lesotho's Traditional Heritage

MUSIC

The Basotho say that Sesotho is a language of song, not speech. The Sesotho words sound like a series of musical notes, and the Basotho welcome every opportunity to sing. Their songs often tell stories that relate to particular events such as weddings or initiation rites into adulthood. The Basotho frequently sing while working in the fields or on construction sites. Musical instruments are seldom used during songs for they are not needed. The blend and harmony of unaccompanied male and female voices creates a beautiful sound. Since the Basotho love to sing, they expect their audience to listen to all the stanzas of a song. Ceremonies in Lesotho have been known to carry on for hours simply because of so much singing.

The Basotho have several unique musical instruments. These are generally played without vocal accompaniment. Girls and boys have their own special instruments. Herdboys often play a *lesiba* while herding their cattle. A *lesiba* is similar to a flute. It is made with reeds and hair from the tail of a horse. A quill

72

A herdboy with his *lesiba,* a traditional musical instrument

is used to hold the string tight at one end and the young boy blows through a hole at the other end. It is believed that the melodic sound brings contentment to a herdboy's grazing cattle. As a result, a *lesiba* is a herdboy's valuable tool. Any herdboy who tends his cattle without this instrument risks being teased.

Girls have an instrument similar to the *lesiba* called a *lekope.* A girl will play her *lekope* when she wants to capture a young man's romantic attention.

73

Traditional dancers, dressed in colourful red and white cloth, with straps of small bells tied round their chests

The Basotho also have a special drum called the *moropa* which they use while dancing. Played slowly, it helps create gentle and graceful movements. This instrument is only played by women; and it is often used when young girls undergo initiation rites.

DANCING

The Basotho have some thirty traditional dances for which they dress in colourful red and white cloth. Many women braid their hair with beads. The men wear several straps of small bells around their chest and back. Their legs are wrapped with flowing streams of feathers, and small tins full of stones and beads are

74

tied to their ankles. The exitement created by the dances is contagious. Soon everyone is involved as they clap their hands, tap their feet, and shout for more dancing. The tired dancers seem always happy to oblige.

Youngsters are taught to dance at an early age. Like songs, dances tell different stories and are also used to make requests. The request for rain is important in Lesotho, since a drought can destroy needed crops. Rain is the source of happiness and luck. When it rains hard, the villagers say the ancestors are happy. A child born prior to a heavy rainfall is often named *Motlalepula*, which means "he who brought the rains with him". Rain-making can be fun in Lesotho. Each spring, following the dry winter season, the *mohobelo*, or rain dance ceremony, can be seen in many villages throughout the country.

The *mokorotlo* is a war dance performed by men. There is much swinging of the body and rhythmic stomping of feet. Often one man will break away from the group and begin kicking his legs high in the air. He may also recite the praises of his warrior ancestors.

The women are not allowed to participate in the *mokorotlo*. However, they accompany the men by clapping their hands and making a high-pitched trilling sound called a *molilietsane*. Women and girls have their own dance, called a *mokhibo*. This is performed on their knees, while their upper bodies and arms sway back and forth. The women and girls sing and snap their fingers, changing movements when directed by the leader's sharp note on a whistle.

75

Taught to dance at an early age, these young boys are performing a traditional dance. Lesotho's military marching band is on the right

CRAFTS

Villages in Lesotho have long produced their own cloth, utensils and decorative items for everyday life. Today, these crafts represent a vital part of the country's living heritage.

Local raw materials are used to make tapestries, pottery, baskets and beadwork. The tightly woven baskets are able to hold water, and clay pots are used for grain and beer. Village children make their own toys, and delicate necklaces made from clay and beads are sold by women in small street markets.

Although both men and women make baskets, women are

76

the traditional craft workers. They learn their skills as young girls in their village homes.

Workshops have helped introduce new technology to Lesotho's traditional crafts. Skilled potters learn how to use a potter's wheel to make a variety of attractive stoneware. Jewellery, which was once part of a warrior's outfit, has been designed to make decorative pieces called *Thebe*. Silver, bronze, gold and ivory are imported to make exquisite items of jewellery. Lesotho's pottery and jewellery have been exhibited and sold internationally.

Weaving is a local custom and Lesotho is best known for its

Women dancing the *mokhibo*—they sing and snap their fingers and change their movements when the leader blows her whistle

Decorated pottery. The potter's wheel has advanced the art of local pottery making

mohair tapestries. The country's high altitude provides good grazing land for the valuable Karakul and Merino sheep and for Angora goats. Women were shown how to use large looms and were taught advanced weaving techniques during the 1960s. Within a short time, this new craft industry produced rugs, wall hangings and other woven objects that are now sold all over the world. The colourful designs are original works of art. They often depict village life, local ceremonies and folklore. Many tapestries carry a design by Meshu Mokitimi, one of Lesotho's best-known artists, whose charcoal drawings are displayed

78

in galleries throughout Africa, Europe and North America.

The Basotho hat and blanket are unique to Lesotho. Visitors in the early 1900s noticed that the Basotho chose to wear their traditional hat over other hats brought in from Europe. The more popular Basotho hat is shaped like a cone with loops forming the top. It is called a *mokorotlo* after the men's warrior dance. Individual designs are often woven into the hats. A second type, called *molianyeoe*, is a flat-topped, wide-brimmed plain hat. The hats are made of flexible *loti* grass, woven onto the frame of another grass called *moseha*, which is found only in the Maloti Mountains. The hats provide good shelter from the sun and the rain. Even Lesotho's main craft store is shaped like a Basotho hat, since the hat often symbolizes the country.

Basotho craftswomen learned how to use looms such as this during the 1960s. The looms enabled them to develop new weaving techniques for colourful mohair tapestries

The Basotho blanket is useful clothing against the cold climate. It is thrown over one shoulder and held secure by a large safety-pin. There is a tradition regarding the Basotho blanket. The birth of a child was always cause for great celebration. Family and friends travelled long distances to bring gifts. Every able-bodied female in the village drew water from springs and wells for the mother and her new baby. If the baby was the firstborn, the father presented the mother with a special blanket called a *serope*.

The blankets replaced the Basotho's original clothing which was made from sheepskin. Colourful blankets became symbols of status. Blankets also play an important role in special ceremonies. On Independence Day (4 October) a Basotho man may wear three different blankets, each representing a special

"The Hat", Maseru—Lesotho's main craft store which is in the form of a traditional Basotho hat

symbol. For example, the crocodile represents the *Bakoena*, one of Lesotho's earliest royal clans, while the mealie cob represents the importance of maize to the Basotho diet. Symbols of a crown and the Prince of Wales feathers are also very popular. Favourite colours include red, blue, yellow and brown. Sometimes the colour of a stripe determines whether a blanket is to be worn during the day or night. A stripe is always worn vertically, because a stripe worn horizontally is believed to stunt growth.

The Basotho hat and blanket are so popular, that they are frequently worn by Lesotho's Heads of State on their visits to other countries. They are also proudly worn by Lesotho's young athletes during the opening-day parade ceremonies of the Olympic Games.

Folklore

Lesotho is rich in folklore. Many traditions have been passed on verbally from generation to generation. Often, when a problem occurs that is difficult to solve, the Basotho will consult a respected folklore expert for the answer. The folklore expert will generally help solve the problem by seeking an answer from ancestral traditions. The life of Moshoeshoe I is frequently used as an example.

Men and women tell different stories, or myths. Men generally tell stories of adventure. With much drama and excitement, they relate tales of brave Basotho warriors. Women speak of legends, with stories that contain a moral for proper behaviour. Children love riddle games, and these are used to help them learn how to solve problems. They are also told riddles in the evenings for entertainment and to help them sleep.

Many of the age-old customs are no longer followed by the Basotho, particularly the Basotho living in the towns. However, certain traditions can still be observed in the mountain villages.

82

Many customs concern the initiation of young boys and girls into adulthood. The initiation of the young is called *lebollo*. Initiation ceremonies focus on preparing young girls and boys for the responsibilities of adulthood, particularly marriage and family life. Basotho parents today believe that it is important for their children to go to school and receive a good education. However, initiation schools are still considered a major part of their children's traditional and cultural education. Initiation rites vary among villages and the traditional education is kept a secret. Once girls and boys complete their initiation rites (which usually take place in their teenage years) they are considered adults in their villages.

Marriage may take place soon after initiation and suitable partners are selected among families. According to tradition, the bridegroom's family is expected to give cattle to the bride's family. This is called *bohali*. Other animals may also be given as gifts.

On the wedding day, the cattle are driven to the bride's village, where the bride's family inspect the animals and make sure that they are healthy. The bride's father kills an animal for the feast which is the climax of the wedding ceremony. The young bride may not smile on her wedding day. She is expected to look sad because she is leaving her parents. Many Basotho couples are later married again in a church ceremony.

When a young wife is expecting her first baby, she returns to her family's home. Her body is smeared with a red ointment, her hair is cut and she is given a special cloth to wear. If she follows these customs carefully, it is believed that she will have a healthy baby.

The villagers announce the birth to the father. If it is a girl, they pour water over him. If it is a boy, they strike him with a stick. The father must then slaughter an animal and a small feast is held in the village.

Soon after the birth, small incisions are made on the child's wrists, forehead, neck and chest. Medicine is rubbed into these incisions to guard against infection. After three months, the father slaughters another animal and the mother and child are then allowed to come out of the house. The child is rolled on

A mother and baby—on the birth of their first child, a husband gives his wife a special blanket called a *serope*

the ground, if possible while it is raining. Once this has been done, it is believed that the child's future is secure.

Many traditions deal with rain, which is the source of life to village farmers. If it rains soon after a stranger arrives in the village, he is regarded as having brought luck with him. A hailstorm means bad luck and no one may work in the fields the following day.

Lesotho has many traditions regarding life and death. For example, when a villager dies, an animal is slaughtered and the people in the village stop working the land for a period of time. The body of the dead villager may only be buried in the late afternoon "when the mountain shadows are forming". The male members of the family shave their heads. A man's widow is expected to wear black mourning clothes until the following winter. She may not remove her mourning clothes in the summer as it is believed that this might cause the destruction of crops in the fields. At the end of the mourning period she returns to her parents' home where her black clothes are removed and she is given new clothes. This change of clothing is called *ho tlosa sesila*, which means "removal of dirt". All relatives are expected to wear a piece of black cloth pinned to the left arm of their garments during the mourning period as a sign of their grief.

When Basotho leave their village homes to work in urban areas, their lifestyle changes. However, respect for cultural traditions is still an important part of their lives.

Lesotho and the Modern World

Lesotho is a country with a rich cultural heritage and a proud history. It is also a poor country. While more developed countries have grown gradually over decades of industrial and economic change, Lesotho's entry into the modern world has happened quickly since 1966. Modern technology has opened up new opportunities for the country's economic growth. These opportunities have particular significance to Lesotho's local employment needs.

The two most critical problems in Lesotho today are lack of sufficient employment opportunities and severe soil erosion. In the villages, a family's wealth is often determined by the number of cattle they own. The cattle are allowed to roam and graze freely. Gardens and large fields of crops are often not fenced, and the cattle can destroy a farmer's cultivation by stomping and eating through it. Overgrazing, combined with the intensity of rainstorms, have contributed to the soil erosion problem in Lesotho. The soil erosion has scarred much of the open, flat

Soil erosion—a serious problem in Lesotho

land, thus preventing major agricultural development. This is unfortunate since agricultural development is generally the key to self-sufficiency for developing countries.

As a poor country, and one that is basically rural, Lesotho is trying to solve problems which affect many of the country's people. Education and health are top priorities. The government is committed to improving life in the villages through small-scale agricultural programmes, sanitation programmes, health programmes to combat disease, and projects designed to help create village income. Practical educational and agricultural skills are being introduced in school programmes to provide young students with the knowledge and capability they need to become responsible community members when they are adults.

87

Lesotho is largely dependent on foreign assistance. Additionally, the country currently imports most of its goods (food, clothing, equipment, etc.) from South Africa. In a certain respect, this dependence has hampered initiatives for self-reliance. It also creates a problem for a country trying to increase its economic strength.

Because Lesotho is such a poor country, it will continue to need foreign assistance for some years to come. Much of the foreign assistance is directly aimed at health and education. However, foreign aid is also responsible for helping Lesotho develop its versatile and expansive transportation and telecommunication projects which are vital for economic development.

In addition to the problem of soil erosion, the steep, rocky

Lesotho's main government hospital—the Queen Elizabeth II Hospital in Maseru. There are several other hospitals outside the capital

mountains are also a natural barrier to large-scale agricultural projects. However, it is believed that other hidden resources are contained within the mountains. Water is one such natural resource. The Highland Water Project, once completed, will have a very positive impact on Lesotho's economy and daily life in many ways. It will help reduce dependence on South Africa for electrical energy, and will also produce revenues from the sale of water to South Africa. Many jobs will be created. New roads will be built, opening up parts of the country that have been inaccessible. Old roads will be improved. Lakes formed by the water-storage dams are expected to be great tourist attractions for water sports and fishing. The dams will also bring much-needed water and sanitation closer to village communities. It is not likely that Lesotho will ever be economically independent. The country is too small geographically. But no country can truly stand completely alone in today's world. It is hoped that the Highland Water Project will be a major boost to Lesotho's economy and international trade.

The Highland Water Project is not expected to be completed until the 1990s. During that time, the country will continue to develop in other ways. New industries will come into Maseru and other principal towns in the western lowlands. More children will have been educated in schools. Health standards will continue to improve. Lesotho has joined with other countries around the world in efforts to combat childhood disease. Immunization against measles, diphtheria, whooping cough,

89

tetanus, tuberculosis and polio are offered free to Lesotho's babies and children. Thus, in years to come, these young children will grow to be stronger and healthier adults than previous genera ns.

Rapid growth s difficult for any new, emerging nation. It is not likely that rural villages will adapt quickly to a modern environment. Lesotho is sensitive to the fact that changes cannot be forced upon its people. Rather, the Basotho will accept changes as they see their lives and their children's lives improving with modernization in fields such as education, health and employment opportunities.

Lesotho shares a common struggle with many countries throughout Africa which are building new nations. However, Lesotho's geographic location is unique. Only two other areas in the world are completely surrounded by one country—the Vatican City and San Marino—both located in Italy. Unlike the Vatican and San Marino, Lesotho is an independent nation. South Africa, which surrounds Lesotho, is currently undergoing tremendous political turmoil and change. Many Basotho work in South Africa, and Lesotho relies on South Africa for many of its commodities. It is possible that Lesotho will be greatly affected by eventual changes that take place in South Africa, though it is difficult to predict in what way. Lesotho was once a place of refuge for people fleeing from warring clans. Today it continues to accept people seeking refuge from a different kind of warring environment. When Moshoeshoe I was building his nation, over a hundred years ago, his primary goal was to keep

90

the peace. Today, it is still important that Lesotho is at peace with its closest neighbour.

Sometimes a country suffers a loss of its cultural traditions when modern technology is introduced too fast. It is sad when traditions which have been passed from generation to generation are treated with insensitivity and ignorance in the pursuit of becoming "modern". Lesotho does not wish to lose its cultural heritage in this way in exchange for a presence in the modern world.

The country will continue to strive for development and prosperity against the background of the spectacular mountains, full of beauty and mystery, which hold the key to Lesotho's colourful and legendary history and traditions.

Although Lesotho is becoming more progressive, it has no intention of losing its cultural heritage. This picture shows Basotho horsemen, wearing the traditional blanket, as they ride to a *pitso*

Index

94